Easy Eatings

The Book for Kids Whose Parents Don't Cook

By Kaitlyn Chee

Illustrations by Jinhui (Silvy) Zhou and Kaitlyn Chee

Photography by Ethan and Kaitlyn Chee

An Introduction
Thirteen-Year-Old Travels The World

Hi! My name is Kaitlyn. I'm a typical teenager who likes to draw and play lacrosse, but most importantly, I have a passion for cooking, baking, and eating great food. Let me start by saying that my parents are not terrible cooks. In fact, they often enjoy the best dishes from around the world. Most of my friends are shocked when they come over for dinner and end up loving at least one thing on the menu that they had never tried before. They start out as pizza and fast food junkies and quickly join me in my love for authentic international foods (and spend too much time at my house).

This made me think—how can I share these experiences with other kids that haven't had the opportunity to travel or their parents aren't master chefs like mine. (My dad made me write that.)

Whenever I'm at home alone with my brother Ethan, we cook for ourselves, since frozen tater tots and microwave pizza get old after a while. Over the last two years, we have experimented and created many simple recipes we can make on our own—many of which are inspired by our family vacations around the globe. As I mentioned previously, I have a passion for baking. Though many see baking as a science that requires an immense amount of precision, the recipes I've provided don't require you to be a rocket scientist (as proven by my brother).

Here's How The Book Works:

I have provided a list of the "essential" ingredients. These items pretty much last forever in your cupboard. I suggest you take this list and head to the grocery store with your parents to fill up your fridge and pantry.

Next, each chapter is centered around a country's cuisine. While some dishes are more ethnic, others have their own culinary twist. Furthermore, the recipes are reduced to their most basic form. However, I have also included some recipes that are slightly more difficult, if you're up for a challenge; these more advanced dishes are labeled "intermediate" in the table of contents. Along with the recipes, are the stories of my travels around the world, each embedded with small cooking tips.

Keep in mind, cooking does not have to be completely precise. Have fun on your new culinary journey and let's get started!

Table of Contents:

The Basics
Key Starter Ingredients for Easy Recipes

Before trying these simple recipes, the first step is to purchase key ingredients that are commonly found in many dishes. These will easily help elevate the flavors of basic meals and can be kept in your fridge or pantry for a long time. Some may sound unusual, but trust me, they will make your food amazing.

Spices, Seasonings, and Dried Herbs:
-Salt
-Black pepper
-Chili flakes
-Rosemary
-Basil

Sauces:
-Barbeque Sauce
-Olive Oil
-Honey

Others:
-Garlic: Garlic frozen in cubes or chopped in a jar are more convenient than regular garlic. Anything to avoid chopping.
-Confectioners' sugar

For the following **Asian Ingredients**, any brand is good. Though the more difficult the label is to read, the better the product probably is. You can find these sauces in the Asian sections of grocery stores

-Oyster Sauce (great to cook vegetables with)

-Thai sweet chili sauce (great dipping sauce for almost anything)
-Soya sauce (tastes like sweet soy sauce and is good for marinating)

For Kids Who Don't Want to Eat Cereal for Breakfast

When I'm rushing out the door in the morning, the last thing that's on my mind is making a gourmet breakfast, but there are a few straightforward recipes I always make. If you have any bananas that are a little overripe you can mash them up and put them in your pancakes. Another idea is to use strawberries to make a compote for the pancakes. To make the sauce, go to the panna cotta recipe in the baked goods chapter. It can be refrigerated with plastic wrap for over two weeks, meaning you only need to take it out of the fridge in the mornings. The sauce also doubles as a good topping for sundaes and other desserts.

If you do eat cereal, cutting fresh fruit like bananas or strawberries will at least make your breakfast taste a little better and healthier. Likewise, with yogurt: if I have extra time in the morning, I love to make yogurt parfaits. If you often find yourself running late, feel free to make this a few nights before. You can simply refrigerate the parfait in a container with plastic wrap.

Smoothie Bowl
How To Make Mango Yogurt Bowls

Smoothie bowls are thick smoothies topped with granola and fresh fruit. This recipe is completely customizable and versatile as the mango flavor and garnishes can easily be swapped out.

Time: About 5 minutes
Servings: 2
Ingredients:

-1 cup frozen mango chunks
-3 tablespoons peanut butter granola
-1 banana
-10 raspberries
-1.3 ounces Greek yogurt
-1 teaspoon lemon juice

Instructions:

Microwave the mango for 20 seconds. In a blender, pour in yogurt, mango, ⅔ of the banana, and lemon juice. Blend for about a minute or until there are no chunks. Since there is no liquid in this recipe this process may take slightly longer than a typical smoothie. Use a spatula to scrape the sides of the mixer if necessary. Then distribute into two bowls. Wash and dry the raspberries. Slice the banana into small coin shapes about a quarter of an inch thick. Top each of the bowls with five raspberries, banana slices, and over a tablespoon of granola.

Nutella French Toast Rolls

How to Make Rolled French Toast

French toast rolls are a way easier version of crepes as they do not have to be nearly as thin but are just as delicious.

Time: About 15 minutes
Servings: 1
Ingredients:
-Two slices of white bread
-1 egg (if you plan on making multiple servings, only use one egg)
-1 tsp milk
-4 tbsp Nutella (feel free to use jam or lemon curd instead)
-1 tsp cinnamon
-1 tsp confectioners' sugar
-1 tbsp butter

Instructions:

Using a rolling pin, flatten the bread to be thinner and more malleable (the bread should be less than half the height it was originally). Slice both pieces of bread in half. Spread a thin layer of Nutella across them. Roll the pieces up to create a swirl that resembles a cinnamon bun. In a small bowl, whisk the milk and egg together. Then dip the rolls into the egg mixture and place the bread on a large plate. After, warm up a frying pan on medium heat with less than a tablespoon of butter. Cook the toast—every 30 seconds roll the bread to prevent burning and to allow an even cook. They should be fully cooked after two to three minutes. Plate the French toast and finish off them with a sprinkle of sugar and cinnamon on top.

Banana Bread
How To Make Banana Bread

Banana bread is perfect for baking on the weekend, so when you're running late on a Monday morning, all you have to do is cut yourself a slice. It can also serve as a dessert, by adding a scoop of vanilla ice cream.

Time: About 70-75 minutes
Servings: 6

Ingredients:

¾ cup granulated sugar
8 tablespoons unsalted butter (room temperature)
2 large eggs
3 ripe bananas
1 tablespoon milk
1 teaspoon cinnamon
2 cups all-purpose flour
1 teaspoon baking soda
1 teaspoon baking powder
½ teaspoon salt

TIP- To make different types of banana bread by adding about half a cup of either peanut butter cups, pecans, or chocolate chips.

Instructions

Preheat the oven to 325°F. Butter a loaf pan that is 9x5x3 inches. Using a large mixing bowl, cream the sugar and butter until mixture is light and fluffy (about two minutes). Incorporate the eggs one at a time. Mash the bananas with a fork in a small bowl. Add the milk and cinnamon to stir into the bananas. In a separate bowl, mix the flour, baking powder, baking soda, and salt together. Put the banana mixture into the butter mixture and stir together. Put in dry ingredients. Only mix until flour can no longer be seen. Pour batter into the pan. Bake the batter for 60-70 minutes. To check if the bread is fully cooked, stick a toothpick in the center. If the toothpick comes out clean, it is fully cooked. When serving the bread, the next day, microwave the slice for fifteen seconds. Be sure to wrap the loaf in plastic wrap or else it will lose all of its moisture. Eat within two days or else the bread will be on the dry side.

Banana Pancakes
How To Make Healthier Pancakes

Banana pancakes are just as fluffy and tasty as regular pancakes but are a healthier alternative. They also are an easy way to use up bananas that are slightly over ripened. See the baked goods chapter in the Panna Cotta section, to eat the pancakes with strawberry compote.

Time: About 20 minutes
Servings: 3-4
Ingredients:

-1 banana
-2 to 3 tablespoons butter
-½ cup pancake mix (follow box instructions) or use the following ingredients for homemade pancakes

-1 ½ cups all-purpose flour
-1 ¼ cups milk
-2 tablespoons sugar
-1 tablespoon baking powder
-2 eggs
-½ teaspoon vanilla extract
-*Optional: ½ cup frozen blueberries or chocolate chips
-*Optional: 2 teaspoons maple syrup

Instructions:

In a small bowl, mash the banana with a fork until there are little to no lumps. This process is easier with ripe or over ripened bananas. In a separate bowl, follow the pancake mix instructions. If you are making homemade pancakes, mix the flour, sugar, baking powder, and salt together. After, in a different mixing bowl, whisk the eggs. Stir in vanilla and milk. Heat a large frying pan or cast-iron pan on medium heat with a tablespoon of butter. Mix the wet and dry ingredients together, including the banana. Optionally, add in ½ cup of frozen blueberries or chocolate chips to the batter. Pour three to four-inch circles into the pan. Cook for two minutes or until the batter bubbles. Flip the pancakes and cook for an additional minute. Take off heat and repeat the cooking process until all the batter is used. Optionally, serve with maple syrup.

Maine
Childhood Stories

In July of 2018, my family drove to Maine. The first day of our four-day stay was for the most part spent travelling. Shortly after reaching our hotel, we set off in our raft, in hopes of catching a fish for dinner. After an hour of floating about in empty waters, we decided

to walk to a local restaurant. For appetizers, we shared grilled octopus and a lobster *tostada*, which is similar to a taco, but the shell is deep fried and shaped like a bowl. The octopus was tender and fresh, and the lobster practically melted in our mouths. Its contrast with the crunchy tostada made a delicious pairing. Our entrees included a pesto *gnocchi* (a pillow like pasta) and bluefish *ratatouille* (a fish and vegetable stew). As you would expect, the seafood was delicious as the fish was caught the morning of. We also ate rabbit *pappardelle*, a wide ribbon pasta. Being my first-time trying rabbit, I was surprised to find that the meat tastes like chicken.

Some signature dishes in the area are lobster rolls and New England clam chowder as fish is such a prominent part of Maine. When I ordered clam chowder, they drizzled bits of olive oil on top, which made the soup even tastier.

TIP: Add a few drops of olive oil on top of pizza or any creamy soup or chowder.

    I also tried shrimp and crab rolls at Two Fat Cats Bakery, as well as a lobster roll for the first time. Even though I live relatively close to Maine, I had never tried any of these sandwiches.

Bacon Wrapped Scallops
How To Make Scallop Appetizers

These scallops are a tasty appetizer for people of all ages. Easy alternatives to scallops are shrimp, fingerling potatoes, and meatballs.

Time: About 15 minutes
Servings: 3-4 (appetizer)
Ingredients:
- 10 scallops
- 5 slices of bacon
- 3 tablespoons maple syrup
- 1 teaspoon black pepper
- *Optional: 4 rosemary sprigs

Instructions:

Preheat the oven to 425°F. Dab the scallops with a paper towel to remove any liquid. Slice the uncooked bacon in half widthwise. After, wrap scallops with bacon and secure the strip with a toothpick. In a small bowl, pour in maple syrup and use a cooking brush to glaze the bacon. Season with black pepper. **TIP: Most seafood does not need to be seasoned with too much because the water naturally makes the food salty. In this case there is also salt in the bacon, so the appetizer does not need any more salt.** Cook the scallops for twelve to fifteen minutes. Garnish with rosemary if desired.

Grilled Shrimp with Mango & Avocado Salad

How To Make Salad That Actually Tastes Good

Shrimp that is seasoned and cooked well can make any seafood hater love shrimp.

Time: About 15 minutes
Servings: 3-4
Ingredients:

Salad
-12 frozen or fresh shrimp (shelless shrimp highly recommended)
-1 mango
-1 avocado
-1 teaspoon salt
-2 teaspoons pork barrel BBQ rub, smokehouse maple, Montreal steak seasoning, or any meat seasoning
-1 teaspoon oil
-1 garlic cube or 1 tablespoon minced garlic

Sauce
-1 mango
-1 tablespoon Thai chili sauce
-1 tablespoon soy sauce
-1 tablespoon brown sugar
-¼ teaspoon chili flakes
-½ teaspoon salt

Instructions:

Scoop out the meat of one mango into a food processor. Pulse the mango until smooth. Then add the soy sauce, brown sugar, chili flakes, chili sauce, and ½ teaspoon salt. Combine until fully mixed. Refrigerate the sauce and cover the container with plastic wrap until the other components are ready.

If you are using frozen shrimp, defrost the shrimp by putting them in a bowl of hot water for two minutes. Peel the shell off (if necessary). Sauté the shrimp with garlic and oil in a frying pan for one to two minutes or until the shrimp is no longer translucent. Flip after about 30 seconds. While the shrimp is cooking, season with pork rub and 1 tsp of salt. Prepare the other mango and avocado by cutting them into half inch cubes. Serve the shrimp with mango sauce and top with mango and avocado cubes.

Mac & Cheese

Elevated Mac & Cheese

This mac and cheese is way better than your regular boxed version, but just as easy and quick to make.

Time: About 12 minutes

Servings: 1

Ingredients:

-¼ cup medium sized shells

-2 tablespoons milk

-⅓ cup shredded white cheddar (Feel free to swap this out for other cheeses or to mix different types of cheese. I often put in ¼ cup of pecorino Romano, which is similar to parmesan, but saltier.)

-2 tablespoons butter

-1 ½ cups water

-1 tablespoon black pepper

-1 to 2 tablespoons salt

Instructions:

Boil about 1 ½ cups of water and salt (does not have to be a precise amount) in a medium pot on high heat. Add the shells and stir to prevent sticking. **TIP- Once the pasta is thrown in, leave the lid on the pot, but balance the lid slightly on the handle so about an inch of the water is not covered. This will prevent it from boiling over.** Take out the pasta after eight to ten minutes. While the shells are cooking, in a medium or large saucepan on low heat, add one tablespoon of butter. Pour in the black pepper. This will bloom the spice, essentially intensifying the flavor. After the first tablespoon is melted, add the rest of the butter. Mix in milk. Turn the mixture off if the shells are not cooked yet. Once the pasta is finished, save ¼ cup of the water and drain the rest. Turn the milk mixture on again (low heat) and add in the shells. The mixture may have separated slightly, meaning you would have to stir the mixture a few times until homogenized. Add in cheese and take off heat promptly after the cheese is melted (about 90 seconds). However, if the sauce seems too thick add in a tablespoon of the set aside water. Likewise, if it is too runny, mix in more cheese. Add another teaspoon of salt if desired.

Turkey Bacon Panini

How To Make A Glorified Grilled Cheese

By adding a few proteins to your regular grilled cheese, you can make a classic sandwich taste even better.

Time: About 15 minutes
Servings: 1
Ingredients:

-2 slices of bacon
-1 slice of tomato
-2 slices of sourdough bread
-1 slice of pepper jack cheese (can be substituted for other cheeses)
-3 slices of prepackaged turkey meat

Instructions:

In a small frying pan on high, cook two slices of bacon for about five minutes, or until crispy and golden. While the bacon is cooking butter one side of each slice of bread. Toast in the oven for two minutes or until golden and firm. Once the bacon is cooked, dry the oil off using a paper towel and slice the strips into one-inch pieces. Assemble the sandwich by layering the cheese, bacon, tomato, and turkey on top of the bread. Make sure the buttered sides of the bread are on the outside, that way the bread will be crispy. If you are using a panini press, cook for three to five minutes. If you want to use a pan, cook on medium heat. Flip the sandwich once the cheese is almost melted or for about 90 seconds on each side.

Honey Glazed Chicken Wings
How To Make Wings In Three Steps

The classic dish is made in only three steps and with only three ingredients. Try using the same honey glaze on any cut of chicken.

Time: About 1 hour 20 minutes
Servings: 2
Ingredients:

-½ cup soya sauce
-2 lbs chicken wings
-¼ cup honey

Instructions:

In a large plastic bag, marinate chicken wings in soya sauce for one to two hours. Preheat the oven to 375°F. Bake for fifteen to twenty minutes. Take out the wings and turn the temperature to 325°F. Using a cooking brush, spread a thin layer of honey on top of each chicken wing. Bake for another two minutes and check on the wings after 60 seconds to make sure they do not burn.

Corn & Chicken
How To Make Corn & Chicken

Corn and chicken is a great option for dinner on the weekdays since this recipe requires four ingredients and only one pot (meaning less dishes)!

Time: About 35 minutes
Servings: 4
Ingredients:

-2 cans cream of corn
-1 tablespoon of canola oil
-1 onion (chopped)
-4 chicken quarters (can be skinless)

Instructions:

Heat up a large pot on medium heat with oil. Fry the onions until they are soft and clear (about six minutes). Then add in the chicken quarters. Cook the chicken until the sides are brown (only flipping once). Add two cans of corn. Once the cream of corn starts to bubble, turn the heat to low. Stir occasionally so that the bottom does not burn. Cook for 20 min and serve with rice (see the fried rice recipe for instructions on how to cook rice in a pot).

Oven-Roasted Mixed Vegetables
How To Make Vegetables That You Actually Want to Eat

This side dish is a tasty way to get your vegetables in for the day.

Time: About 25-30 minutes

Servings: 4

Ingredients:

- 1 large carrot or 8 baby carrots
- 8 fingerling potatoes
- 8 pieces cauliflower
- 1 tomato or 8 cherry tomatoes
- 2 tablespoons breadcrumbs
- 2 garlic cubes
- 1 tablespoon olive oil
- 2 teaspoons salt
- 1 teaspoon pepper
- *Optional: 2 rosemary sprigs

(all vegetables in this dish can be substituted with other vegetables. Ex: brussels sprouts and eggplant)

Instructions:

Preheat the oven on bake to 350 °F. Then line a tray with a layer of tinfoil. Wash all the vegetables. Cut the cauliflower, tomatoes, and fingerling potatoes in half. Regular sized carrots can be chopped in half widthwise. Then cut lengthwise to about how long your pinky finger is. Alternatively, baby carrots can be cut in half widthwise. The smaller the vegetables the quicker they cook. In a bowl, mix all of the veggies with a drizzle of olive oil and season with salt and pepper. Add in two garlic cubes that have been set at room temperature for about five minutes. Then, put the veggies on the lined tray. Sprinkle with rosemary and breadcrumbs. Bake in the oven for eighteen to twenty-two minutes.

Kale Chips
How To Make Healthy Chips

Kale chips are a quick, healthy snack and a good alternative to potato chips.

Time: About 10 minutes
Servings: 2 (about 2 trays)
Ingredients:

-1 ½ cups or two trays worth kale
-1 ½ tablespoons olive oil
-1 ½ teaspoons salt

Instructions:

Wash and dry the kale thoroughly with paper towels. Preheat the oven to 350°F. Then line trays with tinfoil. Remove the stems and spread the leaves across the tinfoil. Mix together the olive oil and salt, then lightly brush the mixture across both sides of the kale. Bake the chips in the oven for about eight minutes on each side or until crisp. Keep a close eye on the chips because they burn easily.

Cheese Quesadilla
How To Make Lunch In Three Minutes

During the summer, my brother and I made quesadillas all the time when my parents were at work. They are quick to make, and you can easily add any leftovers in.

Time: About 3-5 minutes
Servings: 1
Ingredients:

-¼ cup shredded pepper jack cheese
-1 flour or corn tortillas (corn tortillas are more authentic but personally, I prefer flour)
-1 ½ tbsp butter

Toppings: (*optional)
-1 cilantro sprig
-2 tablespoons salsa
-1 tablespoons sour cream

Instructions:

Heat up a frying pan on medium to high heat with butter and fry the tortilla shell. Then layer one half of the shell with cheese. Wait until the cheese is partially melted to fold the tortilla. After about 45 seconds or once the cheese is melted, flip it. Add more butter (about a half tablespoon) to the pan to ensure both sides are crisp. After one to two minutes take the quesadilla off the pan. Optionally, dip with salsa and sour cream, and top with cilantro (either inside the quesadilla or in the salsa).

Nachos
How To Make Nachos

Nachos are one of my favorite snacks that can also double as a delicious meal.

Time: About 15 minutes
Servings: 4
Ingredients

-10 to 15 ounces tortilla chips (enough to fill a tray)
-3 to 4 ounces shredded pepper jack or Colby jack
-½ lb ground beef
-½ onion
-1 teaspoon pepper
-½ tablespoon oil

Toppings(*optional):
-¾ cup salsa
-¾ cup sour cream
-¾ cup guacamole
-5 sprigs of cilantro

Instructions:

Set the oven to broil at 400°F. Then heat up a large frying or cast-iron pan on medium to high heat. Slice the onion and cook in a hot pan with oil. Continue to stir to prevent burning for seven minutes. Add in ground beef for about three minutes or until the meat is no longer pink. Make sure to break up the meat with your spatula while stirring. Mix in pepper. Line a metal tray with tinfoil. Layer half the tortilla chips, cheese, ground beef, and onions. Then add a second layer of the rest of the ingredients. Lastly, take out nachos after three to four minutes or until the cheese is melted. Sprinkle cilantro.

Fish Tacos
How To Make Fish & Pineapple Tacos

These homemade sweet and salty soft-shell tacos are the perfect Tuesday night dinner.

Time: About 15-18 minutes
Servings: 1
Ingredients:
Tacos:
-3 flour or corn tortillas (corn tortillas are more authentic but personally, I prefer flour)
-½ pineapple or 1 can pineapple (about 20 ounces)
-5 ounces cod (can be substituted with other firm fish such as tilapia and salmon)
-2 teaspoons taco seasoning or 1 teaspoon garlic powder and 1 teaspoon cumin
-1 tablespoon butter

Coleslaw:
-20 ounces shredded purple cabbage (or full purple cabbage)
-1 carrot
-¼ teaspoon sugar
-1 tablespoon apple cider vinegar
-1 teaspoon salt
- 2 teaspoons black pepper

Instructions:

In a food processor, shred the purple cabbage if it is not pre-shredded. Peel and chop the carrot in half widthwise. Cut both the halves lengthwise as many times as possible to create thin rectangles. This process is also known as julienning the carrots. Mix together the cabbage and carrots. Season with salt and pepper. In a large bowl, toss the vegetable mix with sugar, vinegar, salt, and pepper. Cover with plastic wrap and refrigerate. The coleslaw can be eaten after tossed but is much better if it sits for a few hours. It can be stored up to three to five days in the fridge.

In a medium to large saucepan, cook the cod with butter on medium-high heat. Sprinkle each side with about 1 teaspoon of taco seasoning or ½ a teaspoon of garlic powder and ½ teaspoon of cumin. Cook each side for two to four minutes. When it is fully cooked the fish should no longer be translucent.

Toast the tortilla directly on a burner on high heat for twelve seconds on one side and six seconds on the other or until golden brown. Alternatively bake in the oven for two minutes at 400°F. Assemble taco with pineapple, cod, and coleslaw.

Corn & Bean Citrus Salad
How To Make Corn, Bean, & Mango Salad

This salad is a great refreshing side for the summertime.

Time: About 12 minutes
Servings: 5 (side dish)
Ingredients:
-2 ears corn or 2 cans of corn (about 30 ounces)
-1 can of black beans
-1 apple (can be substituted for other fruits, ex: peach or pear)
-1 mango
-1 avocado
-2 tablespoons lemon juice
-1 teaspoon salt

Instructions:

Boil corn in a large pot of water for ten minutes. If you are using canned corn and beans, thoroughly wash in a large bowl. Chop the mango and apple into half-inch sized cubes. In a small bowl, pour the fruit in and drizzle lemon juice on top. Dice the avocado into half-inch cubes and lightly season with salt. Combine all the ingredients together and serve.

Non-Alcoholic Piña Colada
How to Make Slushies

This is such a refreshing sweet treat for kids and adults on a hot summer day.

Time: About 5 minutes
Servings: 5-7 servings
Ingredients:
-4 cups canned pineapple (cubed and frozen)
-15 coconut milk (1 can)
-1 cup orange juice
-5 cups lemon-lime soda (chilled)

Instructions:

Microwave four cups of pineapple for two 30 second intervals. Pour the orange juice, microwaved pineapple, soda, and half of the coconut milk into a blender. Blend until the drink is smooth and serve.

Italy
Childhood

In June 2017, my family and I went to Italy. Some key ingredients used in almost every dish was basil, olive oil, and parmesan. They elevated the entrees by adding a complexity of flavor and are commonly used to garnish the plate.

TIP: Topping off boxed pasta with a few basil leaves, black pepper, and a drizzle of olive oil, can be an easy way to make a delicious pasta dish without hand-making noodles. To add more flavor to a standard bottled tomato sauce, stir in a teaspoon of chili flakes.

One of my favorite things I tried was a *caprese salad*, where two of the key components are basil and olive oil. The appetizer is composed of sliced buffalo mozzarella, layer with tomatoes and basil, and lastly drizzled with olive oil and balsamic vinegar. Once we left Italy, my cravings for this summery dish inspired me to try to make it myself. Caprese salad is such a simple recipe as you don't even need to turn the oven on. In my recreation, I used *buffalo mozzarella*, like they served in Italy, but for a cheaper alternative I suggest cow mozzarella. An obvious difference between the two is the texture. The cheese from cows is rubbery and firm, compared to the buffalo's, which is softer and lacier.

The first time I tried buffalo mozzarella was during the third day of our vacation, when my family ate out at an incredible restaurant. The majority of the seating was outside, with a cobblestone wall running across the boundary. The tables on the outskirts of the restaurant were located inside a crevice in the wall, below an old water aquifer; it seemed as though we were sitting inside a cave carved out of the mossy stone. The oak table was draped with a white cloth. The rest of the lawn was scattered with lemon trees that were lit with sparkling string lights. As we ate, the restaurant became buoyant with live acoustic music. Our appetizers were deep fried buffalo mozzarella and zucchini florets that were grown in house. Like almost anything deep-fried, it was delicious.

Italy is not only known for its cheese, but their pastries are also extremely popular. On our trip, we drove along the bright blue waters of the Amalfi Coast. As it was a long car ride, we couldn't resist stopping by a bakery along the way. Our back seat was soon filled with boxes stuffed of pistachio and hazelnut cream puffs, apple strudels, and of course, cannolis. Nothing is better than a crunchy cannoli that is showered with powdered sugar right in front of you. Even though these were the best cannolis I had ever had, the hazelnut cream puff was my favorite. It was the size of a baseball and the fresh hazelnut filling was so silky and creamy.

Caprese Salad
How To Make An Easy Italian Appetizer

Caprese salad is a no-cook appetizer that only takes three steps!

Time: About 5 minutes
Servings: 4-5 (appetizer)
Ingredients:
-1 tomato
-8 ounces buffalo mozzarella (for a cheaper alternative use regular mozzarella)
-8 to 10 small leaves of basil
-2 teaspoons balsamic vinaigrette
-2 teaspoons olive oil

Instructions:

Slice the buffalo mozzarella and tomatoes into ¼-½ inch thick pieces. It is normal for the buffalo mozzarella to contain liquid in the packaging and when you cut into it. Then drizzle with olive oil and balsamic vinegar. Finally, top the salad off with a few basil leaves.

Pancetta Pizza
How To Make Pancetta & Mozzarella Pizza

This is the recipe you have all been waiting for: PIZZA!

Time: About 15 minutes
Servings: 4
Ingredients:

-10 ounces cooked pizza dough (one pie)
-3 tablespoons pizza sauce
-1 ½ cups mozzarella or 6 slices mozzarella
-2 strips prosciutto or 3 ounces cubed pancetta
-1 egg yolk
-3 basil leaves

Instructions:

Preheat the oven to 425°F. Ladle the pizza sauce on to the dough. Cook pancetta for about two minutes. Spread the sauce evenly and leave half an inch to an inch of the crust without sauce. Sprinkle cheese evenly on top of the sauce. Add half-inch sized pieces of prosciutto or pancetta. Cook for about nine minutes directly on the rack. Add an egg yolk in the middle of the pizza and cook for 90 more seconds. Top with basil and serve. Make sure to spread the yolk around the whole pie before eating a slice.

Bacon, Spinach, & Chicken One-Pot Alfredo

How To Make One-Pot Pasta

This bacon-filled alfredo only needs one pot to make and is a great dish that hides the flavor of any vegetables.

Time: About 35 minutes

Servings: 5-6

Ingredients:

- ¾ of one box of spaghetti (about 7 ½ ounces)
- 5 slices of bacon
- 2 skinless chicken breasts (or boneless, skinless chicken)
- 6 ounces spinach
- 4 cups milk
- 2/3 cup parmesan
- 2 teaspoons salt
- 2 teaspoons pepper
- 2 tablespoons of minced garlic or 2 garlic cubes

Instructions:

If you purchased chicken with skin and or bones, remove both before you cut the chicken into two-inch size strips. Cut the uncooked bacon into one-inch pieces. Cook the bacon on medium heat in a large pot for three minutes. Add the chicken for about eight minutes, flipping and stirring every minute or two. Once the chicken is cooked, remove from the pot. Cook the spinach in the pot with the bacon, salt, pepper, and garlic for three to four minutes. Add a tablespoon of water if there is no longer grease in the pot from the bacon. After, mix the chicken into the pot again and pour in milk.

Use medium heat to boil the milk or else it will burn. Once it is boiling, cook pasta for about fifteen minutes. Make sure to be constantly stirring the pot and add more salt to taste. Also, keep the lid off if the sauce is too liquidy, but keep in mind, once the pasta cools down, the sauce will thicken a lot. When the pasta is cooked, stir the cheese in and immediately turn the heat off.

Gnocchi
How to Make Three Types of Gnocchi

Gnocchi is a pillow-like pasta and can be served with one of these three amazing sauces.

Time: About 20-35 minutes (depending on the chosen sauce)
Servings: 4
Ingredients:

Pasta:
- 8 ounces of ricotta cheese
- 1 cup of all-purpose flour
- ¼ cup water
- ½ cup parmesan cheese
- 1 large egg
- 1 teaspoon salt
- 2 teaspoons garlic powder

Pick One of The Three Sauces

Easy: Marinara:

- 12 ounces (about ½ bottle) of marinara sauce
- 3 basil leaves
- 1 tablespoon black pepper
- 1 teaspoon salt
- 1 garlic cube or 1 tablespoon minced garlic
- *Optional: 1 teaspoon chili flakes

Easy: Garlic Butter

- 4 garlic cubes or 2 tablespoons of minced garlic

-3 tablespoons of butter

Hard: Pesto:

-2 cups basil leaves
-⅓ cup roasted pine nuts (do not try to roast pine nuts at home because they burn very easily)
-½ cup olive oil
-3 garlic cloves or 3 teaspoons minced garlic
-¼ teaspoon salt
-¼ teaspoon black pepper

Instructions:

Marinara Sauce:
In a large cooking pot on medium heat, pour in the jar of marinara. Chop the basil into thin strips. Then add the basil, black pepper, garlic, salt, and optionally the chili flakes. Stir occasionally until the sauce is warm (about fifteen minutes).

Pesto Sauce:
In a food processor, stuff as much basil as possible (you will have to make the pesto in batches and slowly add in all the ingredients). Blend the basil for 20 seconds. Add in the pine nuts, olive oil, salt, pepper, and garlic. Blend for 20 seconds or until smooth. Continue to add in as much basil as possible and blend until smooth. Make sure to stop blending every once in a while and scrap the sides with spatula to ensure all ingredients are evenly blended. Repeat this process until all the basil is used. This can keep in the freezer for about a year in a jar.

Pasta:

In a large mixing bowl, mix a ¾ cup of flour, parmesan, salt, and garlic powder together. Add the ricotta and egg to the dry mixture. Only stir the mixture using 25 to 30 strokes with a wooden spoon or spatula. The fewer strokes to combine the dough, the better. Boil the water. Then place the dough on a generously floured workbench or large cutting board. Mold the dough into a rectangle. Slice the rectangle into four even pieces. If the dough becomes sticky, add more flour. Roll all the pieces into approximately twelve-inch long ropes. After, slice the dough into ¾ inch pieces, forming your gnocchi. Then sprinkle a little bit of flour on top to lightly coat the pasta. Cook for about four minutes or until all of the gnocchi begins to float. Mix gently to prevent sticking, but make sure not to crush the pasta. Pan-fry the gnocchi with a tablespoon of butter. Cook for four to five minutes or until golden brown. Depending on the size of the pan, you may need more than one pan, or you can cook the pasta in two batches. Lastly, coat the pasta in the sauce of your liking (not necessary if you made the garlic butter sauce).

Garlic Butter Sauce
If you plan to make garlic butter sauce, (after frying the gnocchi in one tablespoon of butter) add three more tablespoons of butter and garlic. Cook for four to five minutes or until golden brown. Depending on the size of the pan, you may need more than one pan or to cook half the pasta at a time.

China
Childhood

My brother and I went to China for a month-long camp where we, along with a group of students and their parents, travelled through different Chinese cities to immerse ourselves with the culture. For the first two weeks, we were in Beijing  and went sightseeing around the city. As all tourists do, we visited the Great Wall of China. It felt like an endless staircase, but it was worth the exercise. There were gushes of people walking around, but as time went by our group spread thinner along the trail. Once we stopped to get some water, we had a chance to look at the breathtaking view of the mountain peaks. After about an hour of walking, we exited the wall by tobogganing down, which ended up being my favorite part.

During the trip, we often did not order our own food. Instead, the camp called restaurants to order meals for us in advance. This way, we had as much time as possible to explore the cities. Since we were not with the camp during the nighttime, we often went to different restaurants ourselves. My family and I were set on finding *xiaolongbao*, a Chinese soup dumpling, in which Shanghai is especially known for. The skin is pinched in a spiral pattern at the top, keeping the dumpling closed to prevent the filling from leaking. The inside is stuffed with hot soup and sweet pork. It was a little more difficult to find them in restaurants then we expected, considering their popularity, but we were more than satisfied when we finally got to try them. To eat a soup dumpling, you first use chopsticks to place it on your spoon and then you take a bite out of the edge before eating the whole bun. This allows some heat to escape from the inside, without letting all of the liquid pool out.

During the last two weeks of camp, the parents continued to tour around the city, while the kids went to a Chinese school during the weekdays. One place that we all got to visit was a Shanghai silkworm factory. There were thousands of silkworms and the workers let us hold them in our hands. In one room, they had large containers of dye with bright assorted colors to pigment the silk. Next to the factory was a shop where they sold the silk garments. I bought a blue, traditional Chinese dress also known as a *cheongsam*. Dresses and shirts for females commonly have frog buttons and are made of a silk material with floral patterns.

Vancouver
Childhood

Every summer, my family vacations to
Vancouver, Canada to visit my dad's aunt.
Even though Canada is far from Asia,
Vancouver has some of the best Chinese food.
In my great aunt's neighborhood, there are tons
of Chinese restaurants and grocery stores. A
longtime favorite treat of ours is to buy little
candies shaped like pizzas and lychee. *Lychee*
is about the size of a strawberry and has a
brown, prickly shell protecting the sweet,
white fruit inside it.

For breakfast, we walk down to a small, Chinese bakery. The
shelves are always stocked with rows of mango and chestnut cakes,
garnished with colorful fruits; the display cabinets are stuffed with
delicate pastries and assorted flavors of *tiger rolls*. *Tiger rolls* are
cakes rolled into the shape of a loaf of bread, and inside it, there is a
whipped cream swirl. Our family's go-to treats are egg tarts and
coconut buns. Personally, I prefer the tarts because of the flaky and
buttery crust along with the creamy filling.

Another pastry we often get is a warm tapioca dessert which
we get when we eat *dim sum*. A *dim sum* restaurant is a Cantonese
style restaurant in which waiters push carts of Chinese food around.
Dishes range from *har gow* (shrimp wrapped in a translucent, white
dumpling skin) to *chicken feet* cooked in soy and Thai chili sauce.
These classic dishes are typically small but are packed with flavor.
While dim sum is usually eaten in the mid-morning or for lunch, I
can go for this tapioca pudding anytime. The top part has a flaky
crust with a crisscross pattern and the bottom half consists of a

mango pudding with small tapioca balls. When we don't order tapioca pudding, we often get *tofu fa* for dessert—a bowl of sweet tofu with a sweet, ginger flavored syrup.

When we want to eat at home, we go to a butcher shop to get *Peking duck*. The workers pump air into the duck before it's cooked, which ensures the skin is crispy. This inspired my family to make our own Peking duck. As you can see in the photo above, we had to hang the duck in the shower as it needed to dry before cooking. Making our own duck was a lot of fun but was very difficult and I would not recommend attempting it if you are a beginner!

Fried Rice
How To Make Fried Rice

Fried rice is a classic Asian dish that can either serve as a full meal or a side dish. If you have leftovers you can easily add them into your fried rice.

Time: About 30 minutes
Servings: 4-5
Ingredients:

-1 cup uncooked white rice
-1 cup frozen vegetables (for example, peas & corn)
-1 chicken breast, or any leftover meat
-1-2 teaspoons oyster sauce
-2 eggs
-2 garlic cubes or 1 tablespoon minced garlic
-1 cilantro sprig
-2 teaspoons oil

Toppings (optional)
-1 tsp fried onions
-1 tsp seaweed seasoning

Instructions:

Wash the rice and cook with 1 ¾ cups of water in a rice cooker if you have one (most rice cookers have a line that tells you where to fill the water to). Alternatively, cook the rice in a pot. Boil 1 ¾ cups of water with a teaspoon of salt. Add the rice and stir only once to prevent stickiness. Cover the pot and allow the rice to cook for eighteen minutes. Turn off the heat and let the rice steam with the cover on for five minutes.

In a small mixing bowl, whisk the eggs together. Chop the cilantro. If the meat you are using is uncooked, chop chicken into two inch-sized pieces. Then in a wok or large pan, drizzle about a teaspoon of oil. Cook the meat if necessary, for about seven minutes or until fully cooked. Take the meat out. Scramble the eggs by constantly stirring for about 30 seconds or until they are almost cooked. Take them out of the pan and place the eggs in a separate bowl. Put the garlic in the pan and add another teaspoon of oil. Cook the meat in the pan with the garlic for about a minute. If there is not enough liquid, add a tablespoon or so of chicken stock or water. Throw in the rice, cilantro, oyster sauce, and frozen vegetables. After a minute, add the eggs and continuously stir. More chicken stock or water may need to be added again. Cook for four to five minutes. Optionally serve with seaweed seasoning and crispy fried onions.

Chow Mein
How To Make Chinese Stir-Fry Noodles

Instead of your regular takeout Chinese noodles, make your own delicious chow mein at home!

Time: About 10 minutes
Servings: 1
Ingredients:

-2 ounces chow mein noodles
-2 pieces bok choy
-¼ cup bean sprouts
-1 garlic cube or 1 tablespoon minced garlic
-1 tablespoon oyster sauce
-1 tablespoon soy sauce
-1 tablespoon sesame oil
-1/2 green onion

Instructions:

Boil chow mein noodles in water for as long as the package says or for three minutes. Then drain the noodles. Slice bok choy in halves and wash. Chop the green onion into thin slices. In a large saucepan heat sesame oil on medium heat. Add in bok choy and cook for two minutes. Then add soy sauce, oyster sauce, garlic, and noodles. Stir to make sure all noodles are coated for about two minutes. If sticking, add a tablespoon of canola oil and gently stir. Add in bean sprouts and green onions and cook with noodles for one minute.

Tofu Rice
How To Make Tofu Rice

This delicious, salty dish serves as a great pairing with rice!

Time: About 30 minutes
Servings: 4
Ingredients:

-4 ounces ground beef
-1 box or 14 ounces soft tofu
-1 tablespoon oyster sauce
-1 green onion (chopped)
- 1 cup uncooked rice
- 1 tablespoon oil
- 1 teaspoon cornstarch
-1 cup rice
- 1 cup water
-*Optional: 2 Chinese sausages (lap cheong)

Instructions:

Wash the rice and cook with 1 ¾ cups of water in a rice cooker if you have one (most rice cookers have a line that tells you where to fill the water to). If you do not own a rice cooker (highly recommended to have one), alternatively, cook the rice in a pot. Boil 1 ¾ cups of water with a teaspoon of salt. Add the rice and stir only once to prevent stickiness. Cover the pot and allow the rice to cook for eighteen minutes. Turn off the heat and let the rice steam with the cover on for five minutes.

Mince the Chinese sausage in a food processor or chop into very small, quarter-inch cubes. Heat up oil in a frying pan on medium heat. Brown the ground beef and lap cheong in a pan for seven to eight minutes. Add pepper and be sure to break the ground beef into small pieces with your spatula. Cut the tofu into about ½ inch cubes. Place the tofu and green onions in a pan with the ground beef. Flip the tofu once after two minutes. Heat for another two minutes.

For the sauce, mix water, oyster sauce, and cornstarch in a small bowl. Combine until there are no lumps of cornstarch. Pour mixture into the pan with the tofu and meat. Cook until the sauce thickens (about two minutes). Serve on rice.

Hoisin Salmon
How To Make Hoisin Salmon

Hoisin is a sweet and salty sauce that adds a ton of flavor to your ordinary steamed salmon. This dish is best served on top of rice with bok choy.

Time: About 10 minutes
Servings: 4-5
Ingredients:

1 ½ lb salmon
2 tsp hoisin sauce
1 tsp oil
1 tsp salt
1 tsp pepper

Instructions:

Use a knife to descale the salmon skin (if the salmon has skin). Cut the salmon into thirds. Heat a large pan with oil on medium heat. Season with salt and pepper and put the fish in a large pan. Then cook the skin side for three minutes. Cook the side without skin for about three minutes as well. Spread the hoisin sauce on the skin side and cook for about one minute. Repeat this process on the other side and serve.

Japan
Childhood

The sidewalks in Tokyo were the cleanest streets I had ever seen. Many parts of the highly populated city had shockingly few people roaming around. Even in the busier areas, it was dead silent, and the only sounds were the cars passing by. At night, the streets were  illuminated with colorful lights. The backroads were lined with bright signs hung from every restaurant. With such a variety of dining options, on our first night, we walked into a place that caught our eye. No matter where we ate, the people were always incredibly kind to us. However, we did have trouble ordering. While some parts of Tokyo were more tourist friendly, others had very little English in their menus. That night we ordered at a ramen vending machine restaurant. They had a vending machine where you could click the dish you would like, then a ticket would come shooting out with the number of your order, which we handed to a waiter. After a short time, our food arrived. We ordered a few types of ramen, as well as dumplings and *takoyaki*. Takoyaki is a fried octopus ball and is a very popular street food. During our time in Japan, we went to two vending machine style restaurants, but I would consider them to be the two worst places we ate at during our stay. I found the soup to be way too salty, and the takoyaki was not the best. However, I would be curious to try takoyaki in Osaka as they are famous for being the first city to popularize it.

Later that night, we stopped by the 7-Eleven. While this convenience store may not seem top notch, the quality in Asia is very different compared to that in America. Since the chain is Japanese owned, there were many items that could only be found in Asia. Every day, we would stop by 7-Eleven to get an assortment of drinks, snacks, and breakfast foods. While *udon* and *onigiri* (a triangular rice ball wrapped in seaweed) may not seem like a conventional morning meal, eating noodles for breakfast is very common in Asia. Another breakfast food I got there was instant ramen. Surprisingly, it was much tastier than at the first restaurant. The store is also filled with sweet treats like *mochi*, Japanese candies, crepe cakes, Japanese cheesecake, and many more desserts. Japanese cheesecake has a much airier texture compared to the American style because the egg whites are whipped. Many bakeries in Japan are heavily influenced by French cuisine, thus macarons and croissants are not out of the ordinary there. Red bean and green tea are also very common dessert flavors across most of Asia.

Shortly after eating my instant noodles on the second morning of the trip, my family headed to the fish market. In the old marketplace, visitors could see fish being sliced a foot away from them, but the new Toyosu market only allows you to observe from small windows on the floor above where the seafood is kept. The fish market was not my favorite place, but some of the small shops were interesting. There were lots of cool t-shirts and other knick-knacks for visitors to buy, along with an assortment of different types of tea. For lunch, we ate at a sushi restaurant next door. They only serve *omakase* (a tasting menu), meaning the customer leaves the choice of dishes up to the chef. The menu was mostly *sashimi* with a few rolls. He also served us a few dishes I had never had before, like *tamagoyaki* and *uni nigiri*. The tamagoyaki, a fluffy Japanese omelet, was sweet, airy, and served as a nice break from the many slices of fresh fish. Contrastingly, uni, the edible part of a sea urchin, tastes rich and creamy. Not only did I consider this the best place we ate at during our vacation, it was the tastiest sushi I have ever had.

From there, we took the subway to the Harajuku District in Shibuya. The Harajuku culture is known for their popular and unique youth fashion. Harajuku girls commonly have bright and colorful hairdos to accompany their individualistic and eccentric outfits. However, a lot of the Harajuku culture is gone. Most of the shops were common brands you could find in America and you can no longer see many teens dressed in eye catching streetwear. This tourist area was still the most exciting place we went to on our trip. Everywhere I looked were neon colored signs to attract visitors to clothing shops or food stands. While I only tried a crepe, there were multitudes of other goodies for sale, including huge rainbow cotton candies and ice cream shaped like animals. Another craze was the animal cafes. Usually, they have cats or other pets running around while you enjoy a sweet pastry or drink. Also famous in Shibuya is the Shibuya Crossing. This intersection has about 2,500 pedestrians crossing the road at a time, though I did find the supposedly busy intersection not as chaotic as everyone says it is.

For dinner that night, we went out to try *tonkatsu*, deep fried pork. The meat was juicy, and the batter seemed lighter and less oily compared to American fried food. The next day we went to Dempo-in Temple. Similar to the Harajuku streets, the path to the temple was one main road lined with stands. Among the sales for generic shirts that say "Japan" or "Tokyo" on them were a variety of interesting snacks for sale. A very popular dessert is *taiyaki*, a warm fish-

shaped cake filled with red bean, chocolate, or other delicious fillings. We also tried thin rice crackers wrapped in seaweed as we walked towards the main area. The temple itself was beautiful. The different red buildings had curved, matted grey rooftops. Like a lot of sites, we saw many people pray and burn incense there. After walking all day, my family was happy to rest and fill our stomachs with grilled meat, also called *yakiniku* (see photo above). We had an assortment of meat skewers, including duck and beef neck. This was one of my favorite dinners we had because of how soft and flavorful all the food was. We also ate *tempura*, a classic, deep fried food. I personally favored the *tempura shiso* (a Japanese leaf vegetable).

Since we wanted to explore more than just one city, we took a bullet train to Kyoto. While our stay in Kyoto was short, we managed to stop by a few spectacular spots. Fushimi Inari Taisha Shrine was our first attraction we visited. The majority of the area was a hike into the mountains, with almost the whole trail marked out with large, red *torii* gates. While we never made it to the top of the mountain, but the path was still beautiful. Every vermilion gate was painted with Chinese characters. My family even managed to find characters from our own names. Being that my family is always on the lookout for great food, we managed to squeeze in another treat to try here. Like many Japanese tourist attractions, there was street food being sold in front of the shrine. We tried warm, imitation crab sticks. Although they were not a traditional crab flavor, they were still a delicious appetizer before we headed to dinner. The next morning, we headed to Kinkaku Temple, an architectural, off-white building in the middle of a shallow lake. After staring at the temple in awe, we took the subway to the Nishiki Market, a famous marketplace consisting of a huge line of petite shops. Overwhelmed by the enormous number of stores, we slowly made our way down the line, picking up a few snacks on the way. My favorite was a small octopus stuffed with a quail egg on a stick. The fish was sweet and perfectly complemented the delicious and salty egg inside. We quickly moved on to some unique desserts like sesame ice cream. This was quickly followed by mini soymilk donuts and soymilk ice cream. Many stands in Japan make you eat in front of their set up and have a "no walking" policy. This etiquette was developed to show the customers' respect for the food and the people who cooked it.

Our last stop was a peaceful park. The whole atmosphere was very calm and lacked many visitors. Sadly, we were a few weeks too early to see cherry blossoms, but there were still many flowers scattered around the area. There was also a beautifully crafted bonsai garden. Marking the end of our journey, we shared a few bowls of hot ramen before we left on our plane ride home.

Miso Ramen
How To Make Miso Ramen

Time: About 30 minutes
Servings: 1
Ingredients:

-1 pack of instant ramen (will only be using the noodles) or 3 ounces of dried ramen
-3 tablespoons miso
-1 ginger cube or ½ teaspoon of grated ginger
-2 cups chicken broth
-½ tablespoon sugar
-¼ pound ground pork
-½ shallot
-1 garlic cube or 1 teaspoon minced garlic
-1 tablespoon sesame oil
-¼ cup bean sprouts
-1 green onion
-2 pieces of dried seaweed
-1 egg

Instructions:

Boil water in a small pot. Hard boil the egg for nine minutes. Cool in cold water for about three minutes. Peel the egg. Slice half of the shallot finely into small cubes. Heat a medium sized pot to medium heat. Add sesame oil, shallots, garlic, and ginger. You do not need to brown the shallots; the goal is for them to be translucent (this is called sweating the shallots). Cook for about one minute. Add the pork. Break up the pork while stirring. Cook for about three minutes or until there is only a little bit of pink color in the meat. Mix in the sugar. Pour in chicken broth and add the miso. The soup should not need salt because miso has a high salt content. Allow the soup to simmer on low heat with the lid on until the noodles are cooked. If you have dried ramen that is not from an instant ramen package cook the noodles in boiling water for four to seven minutes. If you are using instant ramen, cook for about three to four minutes. Drain the noodles and add them into the soup. Add the bean sprouts for one minute. Chop the green onion and slice the egg in half. Serve ramen with soup, bean sprouts, green onion, seaweed and egg.

Wasabi Seared Tuna

How To Make Wasabi Seared Tuna

This tuna dish is intended to be cooked rare (almost raw). If you do not like raw fish, this is not the dish for you, but if you love sushi, this will become one of your favorite recipes from this chapter.

Time: About 5 minutes
Servings: 3 (appetizer)
Ingredients:

-½ pound tuna
-4 teaspoons wasabi sauce
-1 teaspoon oil
-1 teaspoon salt
-1 teaspoon pepper

Instructions:

Heat up a pan on high heat with oil. Season the tuna with salt and pepper on all sides. Sear all four sides for ten seconds. Then remove the tuna to smear less than a teaspoon of wasabi on each side. Sear on each side again for 20 seconds each. Take off the heat. Add a little more wasabi (about ½ tsp). Allow the tuna to rest for two minutes. Slice the tuna and serve.

Wafu-Dressed Salad
How To Make a Japanese Salad Topped With a Wafu Dressing

This is one of the easiest recipes in this book! It's super simple and serves as a great light side dish.

Time: About 5 minutes
Servings: 4 (side dish)
Ingredients:

Dressing
-⅛ cup rice vinegar
-slightly less than 1 tablespoon soy sauce
-½ tablespoon canola oil
-½ tablespoon water
-1 ginger cube or 1 tsp minced ginger
-*Optional: 1 tsp sesame seeds

Salad
-14 ounces chopped lettuce
-16 cherry tomatoes
-1 cucumber

Instructions:

Mix all dressing ingredients in a measuring cup or small container. Wash lettuce, cucumber, and tomatoes. Chop cucumber into half inch coins. Combine lettuce, cucumber slices, and tomatoes. Top with dressing.

France
Childhood

During my spring break, my parents and I went to Paris. On the day we arrived, we immediately visited the Eiffel Tower. Since the weather was gloomy and humid, we were some of the only people there. The tower itself was nice in the day but seeing it at night was beyond spectacular. If the hundreds of feet of bright lights were not eye catching enough, there was also a color changing beam radiating from the peak of the tower.

The next morning, we walked down the cobblestone streets to get French pastries. I ate a chocolate *beignet* (a deep fried, donut-like pastry) as I sat on the rooftop of our quaint little apartment. If you are a beginner, I highly recommend that you do not try to make French desserts at home. They take a lot of time to perfect and you can't really simplify a macaron or a souffle recipe. After breakfast, we went to the Notre Dame de Paris. Not only was the architecture of the cathedral impressive, the buildings around the church were breathtaking. Inside, the walls are dressed in beautiful pieces of purple glass work. There were hundreds of striped pillars hung from the Gothic chandeliers.

Later that day, we also visited Musée d'Orsay, an art museum. Surprisingly, we enjoyed this museum more than the Louvre. It was less crowded, and, in our opinion, the art seemed just as impressive. Another famous tourist attraction we visited was the Arc de Triomphe. Since France is so well known for crepes, on our way to the monument, we stopped to try some. The restaurant was small and homey. Antique tea plates and oil paintings were displayed on the walls and a little brick fireplace sat across from our table. We had a savory crepe with a fried egg and pancetta, as well as sweet ones filled with tangy lemon curd. The batter was light and thin, and the toppings were just as delicious. The Arc de Triomphe is built at the center of a twelve-road intersection. To get there, we went through an underground passage, which looked similar to a subway. The landmark seemed massive and on the inside of the arch, we saw hundreds of dedications to French generals carved into the stone.

Garlic Baguettes
Cheese & Garlic Butter French Bread Crostinis

These crostinis are similar to cheesy breadsticks and taste good with almost any meal.

Time: About 5-6 minutes
Servings: 4
Ingredients:

-½ baguette (8 slices)
-2 garlic cubes (minced garlic is not recommended because it does not dissolve into the butter)
-3 tablespoons butter
-2 ounces pepper jack or cheddar cheese

Instructions:

Slice the baguette into eight slices with a bread knife. Spread the slices out on a baking pan lined with tin foil. In a small saucepan on medium to low heat, cook garlic cubes with one tablespoon of butter until melted (about one minute). Stir in two more tablespoons of butter. Continue to stir to prevent burning for around two minutes. Add another tablespoon of butter if the mixture becomes much thicker than regular, melted butter. Turn off the heat. Use a brush to butter one side of each slice of bread. Add cheese on to the buttered side and broil for two to three minutes on 450°F. Remove the crostinis from the oven and serve.

French Green Beans
How To Make French Green Beans

Green beans are an easy side dish and go with just about everything.

Time: About 10 minutes
Servings: 4
Ingredients:

- 8 ounces green beans
- ½ pot of water
- 2 tablespoons of butter
- 1 garlic cube or 1 tablespoon minced garlic
- 1 tablespoon sliced almonds
- 2 teaspoon salt

Instructions:

Fill up ½ a medium sized pot of water and add one teaspoon of salt. Bring to a boil on high heat. Wash the green beans and cut the tips off. Boil for two minutes, then pour the beans out into a strainer. Pour cold water from the tap on top of them to cool them off. In a large frying pan, heat up the butter on medium heat. Once the butter is melted, stir in the garlic for one minute. Put the beans in (shake the beans in the strainer until they are fairly dry). Stir around to make sure all the beans have some butter and garlic on them. Add salt. They are done after two to three minutes or when they are bright green; the beans should be soft, but still have a little bit of crunch.

Cassoulet
How To Make Cassoulet

You can easily throw in a pot of meat and beans on a Sunday afternoon and have an amazing dinner, with leftovers for the week. Feel free to throw whatever you have into the pot, as long as there is some type of beans and meat in there.

Time: About 1 hour 15 minutes
Servings: 4-5
Ingredients:
- 3 sausages (any kind, I usually use spicy Italian sausage)
- 2 chicken quarters (can also use 4 chicken legs or 2 duck quarters)
- 16 ounces or can of canned Great Northern beans
- 1 onion
- 1 cup chicken or beef stock
- 8 ounces of canned whole tomatoes
- 1 tablespoon of oil
- ½ teaspoon of pepper
- ½ teaspoon of salt
- *Optional: 4 strips of bacon

Instructions:

Add the oil in a large pot on high heat. Season the chicken and sausages with salt and pepper. Then add them into the pot. Stir so all sides of the meat have touched the bottom of the pan. Turn the temperature to a medium heat. Stir and flip the meat until the sides are light brown or for two to three minutes. Toss in the onions and garlic. Stir occasionally until the onions are almost clear (about six to seven minutes) and add in the bacon. Add the chicken stock. Bring the stock to a boil and turn the temperature down to a low heat for 20 minutes. It should now be simmering. Strain the water out of the beans and add them to the cassoulet to cook for another 45 minutes or so (you can't really overcook this, but the beans may get a bit mushy). Cassoulet goes great with garlic baguettes which can be found earlier in this chapter.

French Onion Soup
A Salty & Cheesy Delight

French onion soup is warm and hardy and is a great go to lunch for a cold winter day.

Time: About 30-35 minutes

Servings: 1

Ingredients:

1 onion
2 cups beef stock
2 teaspoons all-purpose flour
1 slice or 3 ounces gruyere cheese
1 garlic cube or 1 tablespoon minced garlic
1 tablespoon butter
1 teaspoon salt
1 teaspoon pepper
1 piece sourdough bread

Instructions:

Slice the onion into one to two-inch size pieces. In a large pot on medium heat, melt the butter. Cook the onion with salt and pepper for five to seven minutes. Reduce the temperature to a low to medium heat. Add the flour and two tablespoons of beef broth. Stir for ten minutes. Then add the rest of the beef broth. Preheat the oven to broil at 450°F. Continue to cook the soup in the pot for seven minutes. If the soup is too salty, add a ¼ cup of water. Pour the soup into an oven safe bowl or dish. Add a piece of bread on top of the soup and sprinkle cheese on the bread. Broil for two to three minutes or until the cheese is melted. Keep in mind, based on the size of your dish the cheese may melt quicker or slower (this recipe was used on a bowl with about a four-inch diameter). French onion soup goes very well with the garlic baguette recipe seen earlier in this chapter.

Popovers
Garlic & Brie Cheese Bread Bites

Popovers taste like small, bread rolls and serve as a great appetizer or side dish.

Time: About 35-40 minutes
Servings: 4-6 (appetizer)
Ingredients:

-2 eggs
-1 cup purpose flour
-1 cup milk
-1 teaspoon sugar
-½ teaspoon salt
-8 ounces brie or cheddar (sliced)
-2 teaspoons chopped garlic or garlic cloves
-1 tablespoon butter or cooking spray

Instructions:

Preheat the oven to 450°F. Use melted butter or cooking spray to grease a mini cupcake pan (24 cups). If you do not have a small cupcake tray, a regular cupcake tray works too as long as you bake the popovers for about eight minutes longer. In a medium sized bowl, beat the eggs. Then mix in the flour, sugar, salt, garlic, and milk. Make sure not to overmix, only stir until all the ingredients are combined! Pour batter into cupcake holders and leave a third of each cup unfilled. After baking for five minutes, lower the temperature to 350°F for ten more minutes. Take the popovers out and cut a small opening at the top of the popovers. Add a small slice of cheese inside each. Bake for ten to fifteen more minutes and serve. Popovers taste best when they are warm, and the cheese is still melted.

Brownies to Cupcakes
Childhood

With any recipe, you can substitute and add ingredients depending on your preferences and what is available. My family enjoys cupcakes much more than brownies, so my mom and I bake chocolate cupcakes using a brownie mix. All we do is add half a cup of milk to a regular batter, then substitute the brownie tray for a cupcake tray and liners. This creates a denser kind of cupcake, which my family prefers.

TIP: Since we use a brownie mix there is no baking powder in the batter to make the cupcakes rise. However, if you want a classic cupcake that is fluffier, you can add 1/2 teaspoon of baking powder.

I don't usually add icing to these because the cupcakes are so rich and taste better warm.

TIP: If you struggle at plating, an easy way to make any sweet dish look better is to put powdered sugar over the dessert. Make sure you do this step after everything is on the plate.

If you are just starting out at baking, be patient and resilient. When I began making desserts, I would make very small batches, so I didn't waste a lot of ingredients. You may also want to try remaking your desserts that did not turn out the way you wanted them to. Make sure to tweak any steps you think may have gone wrong, like over-mixing or using a stove temperature that was too high or low. Having an over-mixed batter is usually the reason for something having a dense or chewy texture. Other baked goods may also sink in the oven if they are over-mixed.

Four Ingredient Chocolate Truffles
Dark & Milk Chocolate Truffles

These truffles are the perfect dessert for when you want to impress your friends and family, but only have minimal ingredients.

Time: About 40 minutes
Servings: 4
Ingredients:
¼ cup finely chopped dark chocolate
¾ cup semisweet milk chocolate chips
2 tablespoons butter
1 teaspoon cocoa powder

Instructions:

On low heat in a small saucepan, melt both chocolates and butter together for about three minutes or until everything has just melted together. Mix to incorporate and prevent burning. Pour the chocolate on a piece of parchment paper on a plate or tray. Freeze for fifteen minutes. Being fairly precise with how long you freeze these chocolates is crucial to this recipe as you won't be able to roll the chocolates easily if you freeze them too long. Take the tray out and roll the chocolate into four to five spheres. The chocolate is not fully set, so the truffle will likely lose some of its shape. After five more minutes in the freezer, reroll the truffles to ensure an even and smooth shape. Sift cocoa powder evenly on top. For other topping ideas you can sprinkle salt or drizzle white chocolate on the truffles. Feel free to be as creative as you want, or you can leave them plain and simple. Allow the truffles to set for fifteen more minutes in the freezer and serve.

Deconstructed Peach Cobbler
How to Fry Peaches

Peach cobbler is a difficult dish that takes a lot of time to make the perfect crust and filling, but this simplified version takes less than a tenth of the time to make.

Time: About 10 minutes
Servings: 2
Ingredients:

-1 peach
-2 teaspoons cinnamon
-¼ cup vanilla ice cream
-1 sheet of graham crackers
-2 tablespoons butter

Instructions:

Take the ice cream out of the freezer. Preheat the oven to 350°F (if your oven does not have a toast function). Heat up a frying pan on medium heat. Then add a little less than a tablespoon of butter. Cut the peach in half and remove the core. Sprinkle each half with cinnamon. Fry in the pan for one to two minutes. Melt one tablespoon of butter in the microwave. Crush the graham cracker sheet in a plastic bag and mix with butter in a small mixing bowl. Lay the crumble in a thin layer on a tray that is lined with foil. Toast for about five minutes in the oven. Scoop about two tablespoons of ice cream into the section where the peach core was originally. Add the graham crackers on top and serve.

Panna Cotta

How to Make Vanilla, Coconut, & Strawberry Panna Cotta

Panna cotta is like ice cream, but with gelatin. You can also easily switch out the coconut for a different flavor—just make sure to add an extra ¾ cup heavy cream.

Time: About 2-4 hours
Servings: 6-8
Ingredients:

Panna Cotta:
2 ½ teaspoons powdered gelatin or one pack of gelatin
¼ cup milk
¼ cup granulated sugar
1 ¼ cup heavy cream
¾ cup coconut milk
1 tsp vanilla extract

Strawberry Compote:
7 large strawberries
2 tablespoons sugar
1 lemon/lemon juice

Instructions:

Panna Cotta:
Pour the milk and coconut milk into a small mixing bowl. Mix to combine. Sprinkle the gelatin in a thin layer over the milk. Allow the gelatin to solidify for ten minutes. In a saucepan on medium heat, mix the heavy cream, sugar, and vanilla together. Boil the cream (when small bubbles form along the edge of the pan) until sugar is fully dissolved. Take the pan off the heat and pour in the

gelatin and milk. Immediately whisk the cream to dissolve the gelatin into the mixture. If the gelatin does not dissolve, place the pan on low heat so the liquid does not boil. Continue to stir on heat until the gelatin has dissolved. Pour the cream into small serving bowls. Then, place the panna cottas in the fridge to set for two to four hours. If you want to remove the panna cotta from the mold (optional), place the bowls in hot water for fifteen seconds.

<u>Strawberry Compote:</u>
Wash and slice the strawberries. Then, take out a small pot to cook the strawberries over low heat. Cook for about twelve minutes. Stir occasionally and add about a tablespoon of water to prevent burning. As the strawberries soften up, slightly mash the strawberries to create a liquid. However, do not completely mash the compote to keep some chunks of strawberry throughout. Add the sugar to sweeten. If the compote is still too tart, add another tablespoon of sugar. Add a squeeze of lemon juice and stir together Allow the compote to cool in the fridge with plastic wrap (this will keep in the fridge for about two weeks). Serve the panna cottas with a layer of compote over them or with fresh fruit.

Chocolate Chip Cookies
How To Make Soft Cookies

These homemade cookies are perfectly chewy and soft and make a great after school snack.

Time: About 50-60 minutes
Servings: 6 (12 cookies)

Ingredients:
- ¼ cup chocolate chips
- 1 ¼ cups all-purpose flour
- ⅓ cup granulated sugar
- ⅔ cup brown sugar
- 1 egg
- ½ cup melted unsalted butter
- 1 teaspoon vanilla extract
- ½ teaspoon baking soda
- 1 teaspoon salt

Instructions:

In a large mixing bowl, whisk the brown sugar, granulated sugar, butter, and salt together until smooth. Combine the egg and vanilla extract into a paste like mixture. Add the flour and baking soda to this mixture (only fold until each ingredient is incorporated to prevent overmixing). Add the chocolate chips, again do not overmix! Place the batter into the fridge for 30 minutes or overnight with plastic wrap over the bowl. Preheat the oven to 350°F. Take out a large baking sheet. Line the pan with parchment paper or tinfoil. Scoop the batter with an ice cream scoop or spoon slightly larger than a tablespoon, leaving a finger length away between each scoop and the edge of the pan. Bake for twelve to fifteen minutes. Allow the cookies to cool for one to two minutes and serve.

Key Lime Cheesecake
How To Make Mini Cheesecakes

Cupcake sized, homemade cheesecake is a dessert that not only tastes creamy and delicious but will also impress all your friends and family.

Time: About 3 hours
Servings: 12 (12 mini cheesecakes)
Ingredients:

Crust
- 5 sheets of graham crackers
- ¼ cup butter

Cheesecake
- 2 packages or 16 ounces of cream cheese (room temperature)
- ⅔ cup granulated sugar
- 3 eggs
- 2 tablespoons key lime juice
- 3 teaspoons lime zest
- 1 teaspoon vanilla extract

Toppings (optional)
- ¼ cup heavy cream and 2 teaspoons of confectioners' sugar or canned whipped cream
- 12 key lime slices

Instructions:

Crust:
Preheat the oven to 325°F. Microwave the butter until fully melted. Crush the graham crackers with a rolling pin in a bag to make a

powder. Mix the graham crackers and butter together to make the crust. Fill a cupcake tin with twelve cupcake liners. Spoon the crust into the cupcake liners and use the bottom of a cup wrapped in a paper towel to insure a flat base for the cheesecake.

Cheesecake Batter:

Using an electric hand mixer on low, stir the cream cheese and eggs together. Then add sugar, vanilla extract, lime zest and key lime juice. Make sure not to overmix! Only mix until the ingredients are combined, if you mix too much the cheesecakes will have dents or cracks in them once they are cooked. Pour the batter on top of the crust. In a separate tray, pour in a thin layer of water. Place this tray on the rack below the cheesecakes. This water bath will help ensure a smooth surface on the cake. Bake in the oven for about 20 minutes. Turn the oven off and let the cheesecakes cool inside the oven for 20 minutes. Then allow them to cool at room temperature (outside the oven) for 20 more minutes. Then allow the cheesecakes to cool in the fridge for at least two hours. Optionally, decorate the cheesecakes with whipped cream and lime wedges. If you have heavy cream, whip with two teaspoons of confectioners' sugar for about two minutes.